ThinkBetter
LiveBetter
Journal

Also by Joel Osteen

ThinkBetter
LiveBetter
Journal

A Victorious Life
Begins in Your Mind

Joel Osteen

#1 *New York Times* Bestselling Author

New York • Boston • Nashville

FaithWords
Hachette Book Group
1290 Avenue of the Americas
New York, NY 10104
faithwords.com
twitter.com/faithwords

First Edition: April 2017

FaithWords is a division of Hachette Book Group, Inc.
The FaithWords name and logo are trademarks of Hachette Book Group, Inc.

The publisher is not responsible for websites (or their content) that are not owned by the publisher.

The Hachette Speakers Bureau provides a wide range of authors for speaking events. To find out more, go to www.hachettespeakersbureau.com or call (866) 376-6591.

Literary development: Lance Wubbels Literary Services, Bloomington, Minnesota.

ISBN: 978-1-4789-4391-4

Printed in the United States of America

10 9 8 7 6 5 4 3 2 1

CONTENTS

Introduction

Your mind has incredible power over your success or failure. We all have our own struggles in life, and the first step in overcoming problems is to get rid of negative thoughts. If we can't think positive thoughts, we can't expect to live a positive life, because our thoughts will determine the life we're going to live. When we start thinking positive, faith-filled thoughts, we have the power within that will enable us to go beyond the ordinary into the extraordinary life we were designed to live.

That is why I wrote my book *Think Better, Live Better*. In it I reveal a simple yet life-changing strategy for erasing the thoughts that keep you down and for reprogramming your mind with positive thinking to reach a new level of victory in every area of your life. As a child of the Most High God, you are equipped to handle anything that comes your way. To claim your destiny, you need to start thinking about yourself the way God does and to delete the thoughts that tear down your confidence.

This journal companion offers a practical tool that will help you to train yourself to tune out the negativity and to tune into your calling, so you may begin to live the wonderful plans God has made for you. It offers the same encouragement of *Think Better, Live Better* in daily doses supplemented by inspirational and thought-provoking material. You will find a wealth of scriptures, inspirational quotations, selected stories, prayers, and points for contemplation. All are provided to engage you in a process of reflection that will enhance your faith and help you to rise to a new level of being your best.

I am delighted in your interest in this journal. It shows that you want to put your faith into action and reach the highest level of your destiny, and God loves that. You'll learn ten powerful keys for your life:

- Reprogram your mind
- Remove negative labels
- Release the full you
- Think yourself to victory
- Pregnant with possibility
- The promise is in you
- Ask big
- You have what you need
- Keep your crown
- Just remember

This journal is an opened door to self-discovery, so step through to begin the journey toward living the life you were born to live. My prayer is that you will take some time each day to read the entries and to add your own thoughts. But don't rush through it. Slow yourself down and take the time to reflect on your life. Let the scriptures speak to your heart. If you are facing challenges or barriers, there are prayers and inspirational quotes to help remind you that God is with you each and every moment. Be still and listen to what God is saying through these words, then put words to your responses.

This is a journal to record life lessons that you don't want to forget. It could be the start to a brand-new beginning for you. Underline important ideas within these pages, write yourself notes of encouragement in the margins as you read, and jot down fresh ideas that come to you as you read. Especially seek God's help and guidance regarding areas in which He may want to change your thinking. It's a reflection of your life journey. What you record you remember. You will discover that it will bring clarity to what God has done, is doing, and wants to do in your life.

Journaling has also been shown to improve problem-solving abilities. Many people find that using a journal helps them to better assess their thoughts and feelings and to find clarity. The process of putting pen to paper and then seeing your words on the page can help you solve problems while keeping matters in perspective and priorities straight. You may release pent-up emotions in the process, and that is a good thing too.

Be as honest as possible as you write your responses. Don't be afraid to freely express your thoughts and feelings. Don't worry about punctuation, spelling, or grammar when making your own entries. You won't be graded on this.

This journal is designed to provide you with twenty days of daily inspiration and encouragement in your walk of faith. It is best to read day to day in a quiet place where you can meditate and contemplate for brief periods, away from the usual distractions. Take your time and enter your thoughts and encouragements. Once you've gone through it, feel free to begin again. Replenish your spirit and listen for the still, small voice of God's grace and direction.

Let this journal serve as a record of your daily progress and your entries as a testimony of your faith. Enjoy the process. This is your time. This is your moment. You may have had some victories in the past, but you haven't seen anything yet! *1-26-19*

Amen!

ASK
POSSIBILITIES
RELEASE
THINK
PROMISES
CROWN
REMOVE
REPROGRAM
REMEMBER

SECTION I

Reprogram Your Mind

CHAPTER ONE

Learn to Hit the Delete Button

Key Truth

Similar to the making of a computer, when God created you, He put in you the perfect hardware. You're the right size, the right nationality, and you have the right gifts. He also put the right software in you. He programmed you to live an abundant, victorious, faith-filled life. We don't always experience this abundant life because we've allowed viruses to contaminate our software. We have to get back to our original software. When we think better, we live better.

Our mind is like a computer. How we program it is the way it's going to function. You can have the latest and fastest, most powerful computer ever made, but if you put the wrong software in it, or if a computer virus gets in and contaminates the software, it's not going to function as it was designed. The computer's hardware is not defective or poorly made, but the wrong software or the contaminated software causes all kinds of problems.

In a similar way, when God created you, He stepped back and said, "Another masterpiece." Your hardware is perfect. You're the right size, the right nationality, and you have the right gifts. Not only that, God put the right software in you. From the very beginning, He programmed you to be victorious, healthy, strong, and creative. Your original software says, "You can do all things through Christ." He programmed, "Whatever you touch will prosper and succeed." He programmed, "You are the head and not the tail. You will lend and not borrow. You are a victor and not a victim." That's how your Creator designed you.

The reason we don't always experience this abundant life is that we've allowed viruses to contaminate our software. We say to ourselves, "I'll never be successful. I'm not that talented." "I'll never break this addiction. I've had it too long." "I'm slow and unattractive. Nothing good is in my future." Because our software is infected, we go around with low self-esteem, we're negative, we don't believe our dreams will come to pass, and we don't expect problems to turn around.

Here's the good news, though. There is nothing wrong with you. Like that computer, you're not defective or faulty. The problem is in your software. You have to get rid of the viruses. All through the day, dwell on what your Creator says about you. "I'm blessed. I'm strong. I'm healthy. I'm confident. I'm attractive. I'm valuable.

I'm victorious." You have to get back to your original software. If your thinking is limited, your life will be limited. When you think better, you'll live better.

To restore our original software, one of the best things we can learn to do is hit the delete button. When negative, discouraging thoughts come trying to contaminate your software, just hit delete before they start affecting how you live. That thought says, *You've seen your best days. It's all downhill from here.* Recognize that's a virus trying to keep you from your destiny. It's real simple. Delete. Say to yourself, "I'm not dwelling on that. My software says, 'The path of the righteous gets brighter and brighter.'"

You'll never get well. You saw the medical report. Delete. Replace it by saying, "God is restoring health to me. The number of my days He will fulfill."

You'll never accomplish your dreams. You're not that talented. You don't have what it takes. Delete. Delete. Delete. "I am fearfully and wonderfully made. I have the favor of God. Whatever I touch prospers and succeeds."

You'll never break that addiction. Your father was an alcoholic, and you'll be one, too. Delete. "No weapon formed against me will prosper. Whom the Son sets free is free indeed, and I am free."

If you're going to reach your highest potential, you will have to get good at hitting the delete button.

Always ➔

Consider This

The Scripture tells us to guard our heart and mind (see Prov. 4:23; Phil. 4:7), because the thoughts we dwell on control our whole life. You control the doorway to what you allow in. What negative thoughts have contaminated your thinking, and what has God said about you in His Word that will clear out the viruses and restore your software?

What the Scriptures Say

1-26-19

✗ "Meditate on [the Word of God] day and night, so that you may be careful to do everything written in it. Then you will be prosperous and successful."

JOSHUA 1:8

Do not be anxious about anything, but in every situation, by prayer and petition, with thanksgiving, present your requests to God. And the peace of God, which transcends all understanding, will guard your hearts and your minds in Christ Jesus. *amen!*

PHILIPPIANS 4:6–7 *1 26 19*

Thoughts for Today

Good thoughts and actions can never produce bad results; bad thoughts and actions can never produce good results. This is but saying that nothing can come from corn but corn, nothing from nettles but nettles. Men understand this law in the natural world and work with it; but few understand it in the mental and moral world (though its operation there is just as simple and undeviating), and they, therefore, do not cooperate with it.

JAMES ALLEN

You cannot have a positive life and a negative mind.

JOYCE MEYER

Prayer

Eric
1-26-19

A Prayer for Today

Father in heaven, thank You that You created me with the perfect hardware. I am the right size, the right nationality, and I have the right gifts. Thank You that You also put the right software in me. You programmed me to be victorious, healthy, strong, and creative. Help me to learn to hit the delete button on all the negative, discouraging thoughts and to replace them with what You have said about me in Your Word. I believe that because You are helping me to think better, I will live better and reach my highest potential. In Jesus' Name. Amen. *hallelujah!*

TakeawayTruth

Why don't you start hitting the delete button? Quit dwelling on every negative thought that comes to your mind. That's the enemy trying to contaminate your software. If he can control your thinking, he can control your whole life. If the thought is negative, discouraging, pushing you down, delete it. Clear out all the negative things people have said about you. You are not who people say you are. You are who God says you are.

I am → 1-26-19 I am

CHAPTER TWO

Reprogram Your Software

Key Truth

1-26-19

Almighty God is saying to you, "You are My masterpiece. You are one of a kind. You have seeds of greatness. You are equipped, strong, talented, and beautiful." That's what should be playing in your mind. No matter who has tried to tell you otherwise—a parent, a friend, a coach, a neighbor—delete that and reprogram your software. You are not defective. You are not flawed. You have been fearfully and wonderfully made. I am

L ittle children start off so excited about life. They have big dreams. They're not intimidated or insecure. They believe they can do anything. It's because they just came from their Creator. Their thinking has not been contaminated. But over time, too often they get reprogrammed. Somebody tells them what they *can't* become, what they *can't* do. Little by little their environment distorts their thinking about who they really are. Before long, instead of dreaming big and believing possibility thoughts, they think, *I'll never do anything great. I'm not that talented. I'm just average.*

When we find ourselves stuck in these ruts, not believing we can rise any higher, we need to ask, "Why do I think this way? Who programmed me to think that I'm average, to give up on my dreams, to think I can't overcome this setback? Where did those thoughts come from?" Could it be that you have accepted a wrong mind-set because of the environment you were raised in, from the people you were around? Just because it seems normal to you doesn't necessarily mean that it *is* normal. Sometimes we've just learned to function in our dysfunction. *True*

My father grew up in a very limited environment. His parents lost everything during the Great Depression. He had no money, a poor education, and no future to speak of. He had been programmed with poverty, defeat, and mediocrity. He could have settled and lived there, thinking, *This is my lot in life. We're just poor defeated people.* But at seventeen years old, when he gave his life to Christ, he started reprogramming his thinking. Deep down, something said, "You were made for more than this. You're not supposed to constantly struggle, to barely make it through life." He could feel those seeds of greatness stirring on the inside. His attitude was, *This may be where I am, but this is not who I am. I may be in defeat, but I am not defeated. I'm a child of the Most High God.* 1-26-19

Day after day, he kept hitting the delete button. A thought told him, *You have no future.* Delete. "God's plans for me are for good, to give me a future and a hope."

You have no money. Delete. "I'm blessed. Whatever I touch prospers."

You didn't even finish school. You'll never get out of here. Delete. "God is opening doors that no man can shut. He is bringing the right people across my path. I will step into the fullness of my destiny."

My father reprogrammed his thinking with thoughts of faith, hope, and victory. As his thinking improved, he rose up out of that poverty and set a new standard for our family.

You may have been through unfair situations. People have spoken things over you that they had no business saying. You could easily go around feeling bad, having low self-esteem, low self-worth. But don't ever let what someone said or what someone did keep you from knowing who you really are. You are a child of the Most High God. You are the apple of God's eye. You are His most prized possession. God has an amazing future in front of you. If you will hit that delete button and get rid of any strongholds, God will take what was meant for your harm and He will use it to your advantage. *amen*

1-26-19

Consider This

When Carl Lewis was told that the experts said no person could
jump over thirty feet, he responded, "I don't listen to that kind
of talk. Thoughts like that have a way of sinking into your feet."
Later that same year he went on to jump over thirty feet and break
the world record. Have negative thoughts sunk into your feet,
stifling your potential? How can adopting Lewis's attitude help
you to break free from whatever is holding you down?

The best is still ahead of me
you leave me
you brake me

What the Scriptures Say

For we are God's masterpiece. <u>He has created us anew
in Christ Jesus, so we can do the good things he
planned for us long ago.</u>

EPHESIANS 2:10 NLT / 26 14

I praise you because I am fearfully and wonderfully made;
<u>your works are wonderful</u>, I know that full well.

PSALM 139:14

Thoughts for Today

All children are artists, and it is an indictment of our culture that so many of them lose their creativity, their unfettered imaginations, as they grow older.

MADELEINE L'ENGLE

The secret of living a life of excellence is merely a matter of thinking thoughts of excellence. Really, it's a matter of programming our minds with the kind of information that will set us free.

CHARLES SWINDOLL

Our minds are mental greenhouses where unlawful thoughts, once planted, are nurtured and watered before being transplanted into the real world of unlawful actions... These actions are savored in the mind long before they are enjoyed in reality. The thought life, then, is our first line of defense in the battle of self-control.

JERRY BRIDGES

Be careful of "thought life" our thoughts should be aligned in Gods words. I am beautiful I will get through this

A Prayer for Today

Father, thank You that I have been fearfully and wonderfully
made in Your image and that You call me Your masterpiece
and the apple of Your eye. Help me to be aware of any
negative thoughts that are playing in my mind and to
reprogram my thinking with thoughts of faith, hope, and
victory. Help me to break down any strongholds that keep
me from dreaming big and believing possibility thoughts.
I believe that I am Your child and You have an amazing
future in front of me. In Jesus' Name. Amen. *Glory!*

I claim this for me and 1-24-19
For all my children and all my grandchildren too

TakeawayTruth

God didn't make you faulty or subpar.
He created you in His image, crowned you
with favor, and equipped you with talent
and gifts. Don't go through life feeling
inferior, held down by low self-esteem,
addicted, having small goals and small
dreams. That's not who you are. Start
reprogramming your mind. <u>All through
the day, dwell on what your Creator says</u>
about you. <u>"I'm blessed. I'm healthy. I'm
talented. I'm valuable. My best days are
still out in front of me."</u> *Amen! 1-26-19*

RELEASE
CROWN
REMOVE
ASK
POSSIBILITIES
REPROGRAM
REMEMBER
THINK
PROMISES

SECTION II

Remove Negative Labels

CHAPTER THREE

Labels Are Like Weeds

Key Truth

As a teenager, Walt Disney was told by a newspaper editor that he wasn't creative. Lucille Ball was told that she didn't have any acting skills. Winston Churchill was not thought of as a good student and twice failed the entrance examination into the Royal Military College Sandhurst. The common denominator in the success of these people is that they chose to remove the negative labels. Because they thought better than what others said, they lived far better than the labels had read.

I can do all things through Christ who strengthens me

As was true of Walt Disney and Lucille Ball, people constantly put labels on us, telling us what we can and cannot become, what we do or don't have. Many times, these labels are not in agreement with what God says about us; but if we don't know any better, we'll wear them like they're the truth. If we keep them on long enough, they'll become so ingrained in our thinking we'll become what people have said rather than what God has said.

When my father went to be with the Lord in 1999, I stepped up to pastor the church. I had never ministered before. One Sunday, after the service, I overheard two ladies talking in the lobby. One said, "Joel's not as good as his father." The other answered back, "Yes, I don't think the church is going to last."

I was already insecure. I already felt unqualified, and *boom*, another negative label was stuck on me. "Not good enough." That's the way the enemy works. He would love to put labels on you to limit your thinking and keep you from reaching your highest potential. He knows God has amazing things in your future, so he will try to discourage you, intimidate you, and make you feel inferior.

Words are like seeds. If you dwell on them long enough, they will take root and you will become what was said. The only power that seed has over you is the power that you give it. If you remove it, that seed will have no effect on you.

I removed that negative label, but it wasn't easy. I fought those thoughts in my mind again and again. It was like trying to peel off a bumper sticker that has been on a car for a long time. You peel it, and it tears. Finally, I put on a new label: "I can do all things through Christ. I am strong in the Lord. I am anointed."

There was a young lady in the Scripture named Rahab. She was a prostitute. I'm sure many people considered her to be a scourge on society. No doubt she wore the labels "failure, outcast, not valuable, no future." It's easy to think that God surely wouldn't have any different labels for her to wear; she had made too many mistakes. But God never gives up on us.

One day Joshua and the Israelites were about to attack the city of Jericho, which is where Rahab lived. In Joshua 6, we read that when the Israelites conquered the city of Jericho, the only people spared were the ones in the home of Rahab, who had previously hid the spies from the king. Of all the people whom God could have used to protect His people, He chose the prostitute Rahab.

What's interesting is that Rahab went on to marry a Jewish man named Salmon, and they had a son named Boaz, whose great grandson was King David. This means that Rahab, a former prostitute, is in the family line of Jesus Christ.

What am I saying? People labeled Rahab as "outcast, failure, not usable." God labeled her as "chosen, restored, valuable, a masterpiece." When that got into her thinking, everything about her life changed for the better. You may have made mistakes, but you are not what people label you. Quit thinking about what people have said about you. Don't believe these lies. You are what God labels you. God has amazing things planned for your future.

Consider This

You have the power to remove negative labels that somebody spoke over you. You serve a supernatural God. He's not shaken by the things people have said about you. He can do what medicine cannot do. He is not limited by your education, your background, or the family you come from. What labels do you need to remove and replace with what God says about you?

1-26-19

What the Scriptures Say

…you will be called by a new name that the mouth of the
LORD will bestow. You will be a crown of splendor in the
LORD's hand, a royal diadem in the hand of your God.

ISAIAH 62:2–3

The LORD your God has chosen you out of all the
peoples on the face of the earth to be his people,
his treasured possession.

DEUTERONOMY 7:6

Thoughts for Today

Labels start out as little threads of self-dissatisfaction
but ultimately weave together into a straightjacket
of self-condemnation.

Lysa TerKeurst

We inhabit a world in which we tend to put labels on
each other and expect that we will then march through life
wearing them like permanent sandwich boards.

Nick Webb

I don't care what people call me, labels have the negative
value of making smaller boundaries for people.

Michael Graves

A Prayer for Today

Father God, thank You that You have given me the power to remove any negative label that others have spoken over me about what I can and cannot become and what I do and don't have. I refuse to give those words any more power or place in my life, and I choose to put on the labels that You have spoken about me. I believe You are a supernatural God who makes all things possible for me. In Jesus' Name. Amen.

TakeawayTruth

People may have tried to push you down
with labels, but if you just remove those
labels and get in agreement with God,
He will take you where you could not go
on your own. You don't have to figure it all
out. All God asks of you is to believe Him.
When you believe, all things are possible.
Doors will open that may never have
opened otherwise. God will take you from
the back to the front. Don't let negative
labels hold you down.

CHAPTER FOUR

You Have a New Label

Key Truth

There is nothing ordinary about you. You have the fingerprints of God all over you. The Creator of the universe breathed His life into you. He crowned you with His favor. You have a destiny to fulfill, something greater than you've ever imagined. But if you're going to become all God has created you to be, you have to remove the negative labels, especially the "ordinary" label. Put on these new labels: "masterpiece," "valuable," "one of a kind."

n 1 Samuel 16, when the prophet Samuel came to anoint one of Jesse's sons to be the next king of Israel, Jesse didn't even bother to bring his youngest son, David, in from the fields. Jesse seemed to have labeled David as "too small," "too young," "not very talented," and "not as smart as his brothers."

God doesn't label people the way people do. People usually look on the outside, but God looks on the heart. He knows what you are capable of. God can see the seeds of greatness He has placed in you.

After David's brothers were not chosen and he was brought in, Samuel took one look at David and said, "He's the one. That's the next king of Israel." Right then and there, David had to make the decision to peel off the negative labels. He had heard them a thousand times: "too young, too small, doesn't have what it takes."

What's interesting is that even though David's oldest brother, Eliab, saw Samuel anoint David as the next king, he still tried to stick negative labels on him. Later, when David visited his brothers out where the army had gathered to fight the Philistines, Eliab said, "David, what are you doing here, and with whom have you left those few sheep you're supposed to be taking care of?" What was Eliab doing? Sticking a label on David: "inferior, not good enough, irresponsible."

David could have accepted those old labels and let them hold him back, but this time David said, "Eliab, you're still labeling me 'weak, defeated, and inferior.' You don't realize that I've gotten rid of those labels, and the Creator of the universe placed new labels on me: 'giant killer, more than a conqueror, destined for greatness, king of Israel.'"

You may have had negative things spoken over you, even by people who should have been encouraging you. Isaiah said: "No weapon forged against you will prevail, and you will refute every tongue that accuses you" (Isa. 54:17)—that means every negative label. Notice, God is not going to do it. *You* have to show it to be in the wrong. You have to remove the negative label. Nothing that's happened in your past or that was spoken over you has to define you. Even if you've made mistakes, you can show the negative things to be in the wrong by shaking off the self-pity and moving forward with your life.

The experts may have told you what you can't do, what you don't have. Here's what I've learned. The experts can be wrong. Experts built the *Titanic*, and it sank. Amateurs built the Ark, and it floated. The experts said that we would never have our facility, the former Compaq Center, but it's our home. The experts said that my father would never get out of poverty, but he did. The experts said that my mother wouldn't be alive today, but she is. The experts said that David was too small, but God said he was just the right size.

Will you dare to do what David did and remove the negative labels? You are not who people say you are. You are who God says you are. They cannot stop your destiny. Remove the old labels. I'll give you new labels to wear: "giant killer," "history maker," "world changer."

Consider This

In Genesis 35, right before Jacob's wife Rachel died while giving birth, she named the boy Ben-oni, which means "son of my sorrow." When Jacob heard it, he immediately said, "No, his name will be Benjamin," which means "son of strength." Imagine that God is saying the same thing to you: "I am changing your name. I'm placing a new label on you." What would He call you?

Joel's name in son of Strength P-1-49

What the Scriptures Say

Therefore, if anyone *is* in Christ, *he is* a new creation; old things have passed away; behold, all things have become new.

2 CORINTHIANS 5:17 NKJV

"In the place where it was said to them, 'You are not my people,' they will be called 'children of the living God.'"

HOSEA 1:10

Thoughts for Today

Once you label me, you negate me.

Søren Kierkegaard

Break your bad labels instead of living in them.

Orrin Woodward

God can and will break the labels that have held you hostage.

Craig Groeschel

A Prayer for Today

Father in heaven, thank You that You don't label me the
way people do. You look on my heart and see the seeds
of greatness that You have placed in me. Thank You that
there cannot be anything ordinary about me because You
breathed Your life into me and crowned me with Your favor.
I receive and put on the labels that You have provided for me:
"masterpiece," "valuable," and "one of a kind." I believe that
nothing from my past or that was spoken over me has
the power to define me. In Jesus' Name. Amen.

TakeawayTruth

People can call you slow, lazy, too old, or all washed up, but you are not what people call you. Don't answer to their labels, because you become what you answer to. Answer to "victorious." Answer to "talented." Answer to "history maker." If you'll do this, past bondages are no longer going to have any effect on you. As you think better, you will become the son or daughter of influence, the child of victory, blessing, favor, and greatness.

RELEASE

CROWN

REMOVE

ASK

POSSIBILITIES

REPROGRAM

THINK

PROMISES

REMEMBER

SECTION III

Release the Full You

CHAPTER FIVE

Break Out of Your Cocoon

Key Truth

Inside each of us is a blessed, prosperous, victorious person. This person is free from addictions and bad habits. This person is confident and secure, talented and creative, disciplined and focused. But just because this person is in you doesn't mean he or she is automatically going to come out. This person has to be released.

The apostle Paul gives us the secret to releasing the confident, victorious person who is inside of us. He said, "Be transformed by the renewing of your mind" (Rom. 12:2). In the original language, the word *transformed* is *metamorphoo*. It's where we get our word *metamorphose*. We know how caterpillars metamorphose into butterflies. Paul is saying that if you'll get your thoughts going in the right direction and not dwell on negative, condemning, "not able to" thoughts, and program your mind with what God says about you, then a transformation will take place. When your thoughts are better, your life will be better.

Think about the caterpillar that starts off as one of the most unattractive insects, nothing really special about it. But God predestined it to go through a transformation. At a certain point, it forms a cocoon, and metamorphosis takes place. It's a process. Little by little it changes. One day it begins to push out of the cocoon. A leg comes out, then a wing. Before long, it's totally free from the cocoon. It has transformed from being one of the plainest insects into one of the most beautiful, colorful, and graceful—a butterfly. It can now fly to wherever it wants to go.

In a similar way, we all start off as worms, so to speak. Our thoughts, without being retrained, naturally gravitate toward the negative. We think, *I'm not qualified. I'll never rise much higher. I've made too many mistakes. God could never bless me.* Those are wormy thoughts. God has predestined us to go through a transformation—from a wormlike larva that crawls to a beautiful butterfly that soars. Here's the key: It's not up to God; it's up to us. The only way to release your butterfly is to get your thinking in line with God's Word.

What thoughts will keep the full you from coming out of your cocoon? *I'll never break this addiction. My finances are always a mess.*

I'm not a good parent. If you're going to see your metamorphosis take place, you have to be convinced that "In me right now is a great parent. I'm going to renew my mind to get this person out." You may be struggling with an addiction, but in you right now is a person who is totally free. You may be down in your finances. But in you right now is a person who lends and does not borrow. If you will keep renewing your mind, agreeing with what God says about you, it's just a matter of time before that person comes out.

When thoughts tell you, *You're never going to change* or *It's never going to get any better*, just tell yourself, "I'm being transformed." That's how you release the full you. Don't allow the same negative recording to play in your mind all day long. It's time to come out of your cocoon. God is ready to take you to a new level. Now you have to rise up and say, "That's it. I'm done thinking wormy thoughts. It's my time to be transformed. I know I am forgiven. I am redeemed, talented, creative, and disciplined. I am well able."

That's not just being positive; that's renewing your mind. You keep that up and before long you'll release the full you. You'll be transformed into a beautiful butterfly soaring to places you never dreamed possible.

Consider This

One time in the Old Testament, an army invaded Jerusalem and killed the king. The people of Israel were leaderless and didn't know what to do. As they sat there thinking that it was over, the prophet Micah rose up and said, "Now why do you cry aloud? Is there no king in you?" (Mic. 4:9 ESV). God is saying, "There's a king in you." How does that change how you view yourself?

What the Scriptures Say

And we all, who with unveiled faces contemplate the Lord's glory, are being transformed into his image with ever-increasing glory, which comes from the Lord, who is the Spirit.

2 CORINTHIANS 3:18

...that, regarding your previous way of life, you put off your old self [completely discard your former nature], which is being corrupted through deceitful desires, and be *continually* renewed in the spirit of your mind [having a fresh, untarnished mental and spiritual attitude], and put on the new self [the regenerated and renewed nature], created in God's image, [godlike] in the righteousness and holiness of the truth [living in a way that expresses to God your gratitude for your salvation].

EPHESIANS 4:22–24 AMP

Thoughts for Today

Renewing the mind is a little like refinishing furniture. It is a two-stage process. It involves taking off the old and replacing it with the new. The old is the lies you have learned to tell or were taught by those around you; it is the attitudes and ideas that have become a part of your thinking but do not reflect reality. The new is the truth. To renew your mind is to involve yourself in the process of allowing God to bring to the surface the lies you have mistakenly accepted and replace them with truth. To the degree that you do this, your behavior will be transformed.

CHARLES STANLEY

When you come to Christ, the Holy Spirit takes up residence in your heart. Something new is added to your life supernaturally. You are transformed by the renewing of your mind. A new power, a new dimension, a new ability to love, a new joy, a new peace—the Holy Spirit comes in and lives the Christian life through you.

BILLY GRAHAM

A Prayer for Today

Father, thank You that I am being transformed by the renewing of my mind and that the confident, victorious person inside me is being released. Thank You that as I continue to think thoughts that are in line with Your Word that I am breaking out of my cocoon. I believe that there is no limit to what You can do in me and through me when I reprogram my thinking and start believing that I am blessed, valuable, one of a kind, and more than a conqueror. In Jesus' Name. Amen.

TakeawayTruth

Maybe you're not totally out of your cocoon yet, but don't be discouraged. God is still working on you. Every day that you think the right thoughts, you are breaking out of that cocoon a little bit more. There is no limit to what God can do in you and through you, when you reprogram your thinking and start believing that you're blessed, valuable, one of a kind, and more than a conqueror. When you renew your mind, transformation takes place.

CHAPTER SIX

Created to Soar

Key Truth

On the inside of you right now is a victorious, successful world changer just waiting to break out. God doesn't just see what you are. He sees what you can become. People may have tried to push you down, but God sees you lifting up off the ground and soaring. Down deep, start believing that you are redeemed, restored, talented, and valuable. Believe that you can release the full you.

When I first started ministering back in 1999, I was so nervous. I didn't think I could do this. Every voice told me, "Joel, you're not going to know what to say. Nobody is going to listen to you." The enemy would have loved to keep me in my cocoon, thinking these wormy thoughts. He doesn't want you or me to break out and soar and live an overcoming life. He wants us to struggle, to be insecure, to be burdened by addictions and bad habits. It all starts in our mind. If he can control our thoughts, he can control our whole life.

All through the day I had to say, "I can do all things through Christ. I am strong in the Lord." I spoke those words month after month. Little by little, I started breaking out of my cocoon. The first few years I was so insecure that if I heard one negative comment, I would get discouraged. But as I continued to renew my mind and improve my thinking, I realized I didn't need people's approval. I have Almighty God's approval.

What was happening? My wing was coming out. The truth is, I'm not totally transformed yet, but when I compare myself now to where I started, in one sense I'm not the same person. I'm not nervous or insecure. I'm confident in who God made me to be. If somebody doesn't like me, it doesn't bother me the least bit. I'm happy. I'm blessed. That's what it means to be transformed by the renewing of your mind.

There was a man in Judges 6 named Gideon. God wanted him to lead the people of Israel against an opposing army. But Gideon had all these wormy thoughts. He was stuck in his cocoon.

One day the Angel of the Lord appeared to him and said, "Hello, Gideon, you mighty man of fearless courage." I can imagine Gideon looking around thinking, *Who is He talking to?* Gideon was just the opposite—he was afraid, intimidated, and insecure.

But God didn't call him what he was. God called him what he could become. God sees your potential. You may feel weak, but God calls you strong. You may be intimidated today, but God calls you confident. You may feel "less than," but God calls you well able. If the Angel of the Lord were to appear to you today, He would say the same thing he said to Gideon. "Hello, you mighty man, you mighty woman of fearless courage."

Gideon answered the Angel, "How am I supposed to save Israel? I come from the poorest family in all of Manasseh, and I am the least one in my father's house." Notice his wormy thoughts. A lot of times, like Gideon, we do the same thing. "I can't do anything great. I'm not that talented."

Could it be that the only things holding you back from a better life are your thoughts toward yourself? Why don't you get in agreement with God and start believing what He says about you? God sees the butterfly in you. He sees a champion in you. All through the day you should say, "I'm redeemed and restored. I am royalty. I am more than a conqueror." If you keep renewing your mind, you're going to release the full you and soar.

Consider This

From the first time you see the man named Jacob in Genesis 25, you see that he was dishonest, a cheater and a deceiver, full of flaws. Over the years, God kept working on Jacob, making him and molding him. In Genesis 32, we read that God culminated the transformation of Jacob by changing his name from a deceiver to "a prince"? How can the king or the queen whom God has put in you be released?

What the Scriptures Say

Moses said to the LORD, "Pardon your servant, Lord. I have never been eloquent, neither in the past nor since you have spoken to your servant. I am slow of speech and tongue."
The LORD said to him, "Who gave human beings their mouths? Who makes them deaf or mute? Who gives them sight or makes them blind? Is it not I, the LORD? Now go; I will help you speak and will teach you what to say."

EXODUS 4:10–12

...but those who hope in the LORD will renew their strength. They will soar on wings like eagles; they will run and not grow weary, they will walk and not be faint.

ISAIAH 40:31

Thoughts for Today

The only place where your dream becomes impossible
is in your own thinking.

Robert H. Schuller

I would rather be what God chose to make me than the
most glorious creature that I could think of; for to have
been thought about, born in God's thought, and then
made by God, is the dearest, grandest, and most
precious thing in all thinking.

George MacDonald

Faith does not operate in the realm of the possible. There
is no glory for God in that which is humanly possible.
Faith begins where man's power ends.

George Müller

A Prayer for Today

Father God, thank You that the transformation has
started in my life and that the butterfly in me is coming out.
You have redeemed and restored me and made me more
than a conqueror. Thank You that You are bringing out the
champion in me and that as I continue to renew my mind
I will release the full me and soar. I believe that You
created me to soar to places I could never have
gone on my own. In Jesus' Name. Amen.

TakeawayTruth

Today is going to be the start of a transformation in your life. Some metamorphosis is about to take place. God doesn't want you to stay in your cocoon. He created you to soar. Keep thinking better thoughts. You're not going to stay where you are. The butterfly in you is coming out. You're going to soar to places that you could never have gone on your own. You're going to release the full you.

ASK

POSSIBILITIES

THINK

PROMISES

REPROGRAM

REMEMBER

RELEASE

CROWN

REMOVE

Think Yourself to Victory

CHAPTER SEVEN

Fix Your Thoughts on God

Key Truth

The Scripture tells us to *meditate*, "to think about over and over," on God's promises. You need to pay attention to your thoughts, because when you worry, you're meditating on the wrong thing and using your faith in reverse. If you go through the day worried about your finances, family, and future, it's going to cause you to be anxious, fearful, negative, and discouraged.

Y ou control the doorway to your mind. The whole issue is what you're choosing to meditate on. Philippians 4:8 says, "Whatever is true, whatever is noble, whatever is right, whatever is pure, whatever is lovely, whatever is admirable—if anything is excellent or praiseworthy—think about such things." If it's not a good report, don't dwell on it, because it's going to poison your spirit. Instead of replaying today's doom and gloom over and over, replay what God says. Yes, the economy may be a little shaky, but God says He will supply all your needs. He said He will prosper you even in a time of famine. He said He will open the windows of heaven and pour out blessings that you cannot contain. Go through the day meditating on that!

King David said, "Some trust in chariots and some in horses, but we trust in the name of the Lord our God" (Ps. 20:7). In modern times, he might say, "Some trust in their money, in their job, in what the economists say. But our trust is in Jehovah Jireh, the Lord our Provider." When you meditate on that, you know God is in control, and He can give you total victory. But it all depends on what's going on in your thought life. You can meditate on the problem or you can meditate on the promises. You can meditate on the news report or you can meditate on God's report. What you allow to play in your mind will determine what kind of life you live. When you think better, you will live better.

Isaiah said about God, "You will keep in perfect peace those whose minds are steadfast, because they trust in you" (Isa. 26:3). Notice there is a way not only to have peace but to have perfect peace. How? Keep your thoughts fixed on Him. Pay attention to what is playing in your mind. You can't go through the day thinking, *I hope my child straightens up.* Or, *What's going to happen if I get laid off?* Or, *I might not overcome this illness.* When you dwell on thoughts such as these, you're not going to have peace. Meditating on the problem doesn't make it better; it makes it worse. You have to change what you're dwelling on. All through the day, go around thinking, *God has me in the palm of His hand. All things work together for my good. This problem didn't come to stay, it came to pass. Many are the afflictions of the righteous, but the Lord delivers me out of them all.* That's thinking better. When you meditate on that, you'll have greater peace, greater joy, and greater strength.

Some people have thought themselves depressed. They have focused on their problems for so long they've thought themselves discouraged. The good news is that you can also think yourself happy. You can think yourself peaceful. You can even think yourself into a better mood.

The Scripture tells us, "Arise [from spiritual depression to a new life], shine [be radiant with the glory *and* brilliance of the LORD]" (Isa. 60:1 AMP). The first place in which we have to arise is our thinking. You have to put on a new attitude with better thoughts. Don't go through the day thinking about your problems, dwelling on who hurt you. That's going to keep you discouraged. You need to start thinking yourself happy.

Consider This

The apostle Paul said, "I think myself happy" (Acts 26:2 NKJV), even though it involved defending the gospel before King Agrippa, for which he was imprisoned and could die. Happiness starts in our thinking. Paul was saying, "It may look bad, but my mind is filled with thoughts of hope, faith, and victory." What are some ways that you can think yourself happy and be at peace?

What the Scriptures Say

Therefore if you have been raised with Christ [to a new life, sharing in His resurrection from the dead], keep seeking the things that are above, where Christ is, seated at the right hand of God. Set your mind *and* keep focused *habitually* on the things above [the heavenly things], not on things that are on the earth [which have only temporal value].

COLOSSIANS 3:1–2 AMP

My son, pay attention to what I say; turn your ear to my words. Do not let them out of your sight, keep them within your heart; for they are life to those who find them and health to one's whole body.

PROVERBS 4:20–22

Thoughts for Today

Your life today is a result of your thinking yesterday. Your life tomorrow will be determined by what you think today.

JOHN MAXWELL

We can have the mind of Christ when we meditate on the Word of God.

CRYSTAL MCDOWELL

An unschooled man who knows how to meditate upon the Lord has learned far more than the man with the highest education who does not know how to meditate.

CHARLES STANLEY

A Prayer for Today

Father in heaven, thank You for the amazing promise that
You will keep me in perfect peace when my mind is steadfastly
trusting in You. Thank You that I can think myself happy
by meditating upon the promises in Your Word. I believe
that this is going to be a great day, that something
good is going to happen to me today, because You
have made this day. In Jesus' Name. Amen.

TakeawayTruth

Don't ever start the day in neutral. If
you start it negative, discouraged, and
complaining, you are setting the tone for
a lousy day. You have to get your mind
going in the right direction. Your life
is going to follow your thoughts. Start
your day declaring, "This is going to be
a great day. This is the day that the Lord
has made. I'm excited about my future.
Something good is going to happen to
me today."

CHAPTER EIGHT

Become What You Believe

Key Truth

When you meditate on God's promises, have your mind filled with God's Word, and know His thoughts toward you, the Creator of the universe goes to work. When you're in agreement with God, He will cause His favor to shine down on you. The bottom line is that when your thoughts are fixed on Him, you're going to become what you believe.

Jesus said to two blind men whom He healed, "Become what you believe" (Matt. 9:29 MSG). If you believe you'll never meet the right person and get married, unfortunately, you probably won't. Your faith is working. If you believe you'll never get out of debt, you won't. If you believe you're going to get laid off, don't be surprised if you do. You're going to become what you believe. I'm asking you to believe what God says about you. Believe that you are blessed. Believe that your best days are in front of you. Believe that you're strong, healthy, talented, creative, and well able. Get rid of those wrong thoughts that are contaminating your thinking, and start meditating on what God says about you.

The Message Bible translation of Psalm 1 says that when you meditate on God's Word day and night, "You're a tree...bearing fresh fruit every month, never dropping a leaf, always in blossom." Notice that it is not in some months but in every month of your life. That means even if the economy goes down, you'll still be bearing fruit. It means that when others are going under, you'll be going over. When others have fear, you'll have peace. When others are complaining, you'll have a song of praise. When others are surviving, you'll be thriving.

That's God's dream for your life—that you're "always in blossom," that you're always in peace, that you're always excited about your future. And no, it doesn't mean that we'll never have adversities. But in those difficult times, because you have your thoughts fixed on Him, deep down there will be a confidence, a knowing that everything is going to be all right. You will know that God is still on the throne. He is fighting your battles, and you're not only going to come out, you're going to come out better off than you were before.

Take inventory of what's playing in your mind. I'm not saying to deny the negative reports that are true and to act as though they don't exist. I'm simply saying: Don't dwell on them. Don't let them consume you to where that's all you think and talk about. Learn to put things in perspective.

Once in the Scripture, Jesus was on His way to pray for a person who was very sick when people approached and said, "Tell Jesus it's too late. The person has already died." We are told that Jesus overheard but ignored the negative report (see Mark 5:36 AMPC). He didn't let it take root, meditate on it, or get discouraged and go back home. He also didn't deny that the report was true or pretend the person had not died.

Jesus knew that people don't have the final say. God has the final say. Sometimes in order to stay in faith you have to ignore a negative report. You have to ignore what somebody said about you. You have to ignore what your own thoughts are telling you. You may hear it, but you can do like Jesus and choose not to dwell on it, choose to believe a better report. If you will get in agreement with God and not let those distractions pull you off course, God will get you to where He wants you to be.

Consider This

Job said, "The thing I greatly feared has come upon me" (Job 3:25 NKJV). Just as our faith can work in the right direction, it can work in the wrong direction. Identify the areas of your thinking where you are most vulnerable to drawing in what is negative and describe how you can fill your mind with the right thoughts.

What the Scriptures Say

Let the [spoken] word of Christ have its home within
you [dwelling in your heart and mind—permeating every
aspect of your being] as you teach [spiritual things]
and admonish *and* train one another with all wisdom,
singing psalms and hymns and spiritual songs with
thankfulness in your hearts to God.

COLOSSIANS 3:16 AMP

The LORD of Heaven's Armies has sworn this oath: "It will all
happen as I have planned. It will be as I have decided."

ISAIAH 14:24 NLT

Thoughts for Today

Faith is not shelter against difficulties, but belief in
the face of all contradictions.

PAUL TOURNIER

Seek not to understand that you may believe, but believe
that you may understand.

AUGUSTINE

Faith is the subtle chain that binds us to the infinite.

O. E. SMITH

A Prayer for Today

Father, thank You that as I meditate on Your Word,
You will cause me to bear fresh fruit every month and to
always be in blossom. Help me to never dwell on negative
reports, but to believe better reports, because people don't
have the final say in my life; You do. I believe that as I
focus my thoughts on what You say about me, I will
become what I believe. In Jesus' Name. Amen.

TakeawayTruth

Friend, the first place we win the victory
is in our own thinking. There will be times
when it feels as though every voice is
telling you, "You can't do it. You'll never
overcome this problem." If you'll keep
your thoughts fixed on what God says,
you will overcome the obstacles and
accomplish your dreams. Purposefully
think power thoughts: *I'm strong. I'm
talented. I'm creative. I have the favor of
God.* Remember, you're going to become
what you believe.

RELEASE

CROWN

REMOVE

ASK

POSSIBILITIES

THINK

PROMISES

REPROGRAM

REMEMBER

Pregnant with Possibility

CHAPTER NINE

Something Is Kicking on the Inside

Key Truth

Early in a pregnancy, a woman shows no sign that she's going to have a baby. But on the inside a seed has taken root. Later, she'll start gaining weight, then she'll feel something kicking on the inside. In a similar way, you are pregnant. God has placed all kinds of potential in you—gifts, talents, ideas, dreams, healing, increase, and freedom. The seed God put in you has already taken root. Your time is coming to give birth to it.

salm 7:14 NLT says the ungodly "are pregnant with trouble and give birth to lies." The good news is: That's not you. You are the righteous. You're not pregnant with trouble, with bad breaks, or lack. Whether you realize it or not, you are pregnant with favor, with talent, with possibilities, with victory. Just because you don't see anything happening doesn't mean it's not going to come to pass. The seed God put in you has already taken root. Conception has occurred.

Instead of being discouraged and thinking, *It's never going to happen. It's been so long. I've been through too much,* all through the day, keep saying, "Lord, I thank You that I'm pregnant with Your promises, that I will give birth to everything You've put in me." You may not see any changes. It may not look in the natural as though it's ever going to work out, but deep down in your spirit, you choose to believe that conception has occurred. In God's perfect timing, when everything is ready, you're going to give birth.

Your family may be struggling with dysfunction in your home. Don't live worried. You are pregnant with restoration, pregnant with the breakthrough. Maybe business is slow and you lost your main client. You could easily be discouraged, but you can feel something kicking on the inside, something saying, "Whatever you touch will prosper and succeed." Perhaps your dream looks impossible. It's been a long time, you gave it your best effort, and it didn't work out; but deep down you can't help it—something keeps kicking, telling you that it's still on the way. What God started, He will finish.

In the Scripture, Sarah was over ninety years old when she gave birth to Isaac. This is way too old in the natural, but we serve a supernatural God. He can make a way where you don't see a way. Don't abort your baby. Don't talk yourself out of your dreams. Don't give up on what God promised you. You can still give birth. You can still meet the right person, still start your own business, still go to college, still break the addiction. That seed is alive in you.

Here's the key: You can't judge what's in you by what's around you. All of Sarah's circumstances said, "You'll be barren your whole life. You're too old. No woman your age has babies. It's impossible." If she had believed that lie and let that seed take root, the miracle birth would never have happened. You can draw in the negative with your doubt or you can draw in God's blessings with your faith. Don't let what you see around you cause you to give up on your dreams.

You may be in some kind of limited environment today, with nothing inspiring around you. In the natural, there's no obvious way that you can become successful, but what's around you does not determine what God put in you. You have seeds of greatness. You are pregnant with success, pregnant with ability, pregnant with talent. God did not create anyone in whom He did not put something significant on the inside. Your attitude should be, *I can feel something kicking on the inside. I know something good is growing. I'm going to give birth to what God put in me.*

Consider This

What do you believe God has placed inside you?
What is He bringing to birth in and through your life?
At what stage would you say you are at in your pregnancy?
Do you see signs that it is coming to pass?

What the Scriptures Say

...being confident of this, that he who began a good work in you will carry it on to completion until the day of Christ Jesus.

PHILIPPIANS 1:6

Now to him who is able to do immeasurably more than all we ask or imagine, according to his power that is at work within us...

EPHESIANS 3:20

Thoughts for Today

Everyone has inside of him a piece of good news.
The good news is that you don't know how great you can be!
How much you can love! What you can accomplish!
And what your potential is!

ANNE FRANK

What you believe is very powerful. If you have toxic
emotions of fear, guilt, and depression, it is because you
have wrong thinking, and you have wrong thinking
because of wrong believing.

JOSEPH PRINCE

Alleged "impossibilities" are opportunities for our
capacities to be stretched.

CHARLES SWINDOLL

A Prayer for Today

Father God, thank You that You placed all kinds of
potential in me—gifts, talents, ideas, dreams, healing,
increase, and freedom. Thank You that the seed You put in
me has already taken root, and that in Your perfect timing
I will give birth to it. Whether or not I see any changes
in my life today, I believe that what You started,
You will finish. In Jesus' Name. Amen.

TakeawayTruth

When you get quiet, alone at night, when it's just you and God, if you listen carefully, you'll hear something whispering, "This is not your destiny. You were made for more." What is that? That's your baby kicking. It's because you're going to give birth. You're going to see supernatural opportunities, explosive blessings, and divine connections. God is going to help you go where you could not go on your own.

CHAPTER TEN

Recognize the True Labor Pains

Key Truth

"Well, Joel, I believe I'm pregnant. I have big dreams, and I'm standing on God's promises, but everything is coming against me. It seems as though the more I pray, the worse it gets. I'm doing the right thing, but the wrong thing is happening." Here's the beauty: Pain is a sign that you're about to give birth. Trouble, difficulties, being uncomfortable—those are signs that you're getting closer.

When Victoria was pregnant with our two children, the first couple months were no big deal, everything was fine. But about seven or eight months in, her back began hurting, her feet started swelling, and she couldn't sleep well at night. The longer she was pregnant, the more uncomfortable she became. When she went into labor, I was in the delivery room right next to her bed, and she had her hand on my bicep. When she had a contraction, it would hurt so badly she would squeeze my arm as hard as she could. She would scream, then I would scream. The closer she got to the birth, the more painful it was.

It is during the tough times that many people abort their dreams, thinking, *I knew it wouldn't work out. The bank turned me down. The medical report wasn't good. I didn't get the promotion.* Recognize that those are labor pains. When everything comes against you—your child's acting up, trouble at work, setbacks in your finances—don't get discouraged. You're about to give birth. You're getting closer. You're about to see a promise come to pass. Stay in faith. Keep doing the right thing. The birth is on the way.

Stephen King had a dream to become a writer, but he was so poor he had to borrow a suit and tie for his wedding. He and his wife had a newborn baby, and they were living in an old, run-down trailer. He drove a rusted-out car that was held together with wire and duct tape. In the summers, during the day he worked for a laundry company, making sixty dollars a week. At night, he worked as a janitor, cleaning offices. When he wasn't working, he would spend hour after hour writing fiction stories in their small laundry room. He sent manuscripts of his novels to different publishers and agents, but every one of them was rejected. He didn't even know if people were actually reading them. He began writing one final story, but he was so discouraged that he threw the manuscript in the trash. His wife came home and found it crumpled up in the garbage, took it out, and eventually they sent that story to a different publisher. This time the publisher responded and offered him a contract. That story went on to sell over five million books. In 1976, it was made into a movie and became one of the top-grossing films of the year.

Like him, you may be pregnant with a book, pregnant with a career, pregnant with a business, or pregnant with a charity. You've had disappointments—you tried and it didn't work out—but you can still feel the kicking on the inside. You can't get away from it. Don't talk yourself out of it. It's all a part of the process. Keep trying, keep believing, keep doing everything you can, and at the right time you will give birth. The right people, the right opportunities, and the right breaks will show up. You can't make it happen on your own; it will be the hand of God. What He's put in you is going to be bigger than you could have imagined, better than anything you've ever dreamed, and more rewarding than you ever thought possible.

Consider This

Sarah was eighty years old and had never had a baby when God told Abraham he would have a son as an heir (see Gen. 15). Everywhere she looked, she couldn't find another eighty-year-old woman who had ever had a baby that would encourage her to believe that God could also do it for her. When you look around, are there examples of other people who birthed a dream similar to yours? What encouragement can you draw in from them? What if you can't find any examples?

What the Scriptures Say

My little children, for whom I am again in [the pains of]
labor until Christ is [completely and permanently]
formed within you...

GALATIANS 4:19 AMP

And because the gracious hand of my God was on me,
the king granted my requests.

NEHEMIAH 2:8

Thoughts for Today

God will not permit any troubles to come upon us,
unless He has a specific plan by which great blessing
can come out of the difficulty.

PETER MARSHALL

All our difficulties are only platforms for the manifestations
of God's grace, power, and love.

HUDSON TAYLOR

Never give up, for that is just the place and time
that the tide will turn.

HARRIET BEECHER STOWE

....
....
....
....
....
....
....
....
....
....
....
....
....

A Prayer for Today

Father in heaven, thank You for the dreams that You have put into my heart and the promises You have given to me in Your Word. Thank You that I can stay in faith and keep doing the right thing when difficulties, troubles, and disappointments come against me. I believe that You are bringing me to a new level of my destiny and that I am about to give birth to something greater. In Jesus' Name. Amen.

TakeawayTruth

Sometimes what we think is a setback
is really just labor pains. That difficulty
you're facing is not the end; it's a part of
the birthing process. You're about to step
into a new level of your destiny. Don't
be discouraged by the disappointment,
the closed door, or the bad break. That's
a sign you're about to give birth to
something greater.

RELEASE
ASK
POSSIBILITIES
CROWN
REMOVE
THINK
PROMISES
REPROGRAM
REMEMBER

SECTION VI

The Promise Is in You

CHAPTER ELEVEN

The Promise Comes through You

Key Truth

So often, we look at others and think, *Wow, they are so amazing, smart, beautiful, and I am so ordinary.* You have to realize there's something amazing about you as well. You have been fearfully and wonderfully made. You didn't get left out when God was handing out the gifts, the talents, or the looks. He put something special in you that will cause you to shine.

For many years, I cheered my father on. I'd see my father speaking to thousands of people, making a difference, doing something great. In the back of my mind, I thought, *I could never do that. He's so gifted. He's so talented.* After I came back from college, I worked for seventeen years behind the scenes at the church with my parents, doing the television production and doing my best to make my father look good.

As my father got older, people would ask, "Joel, what's going to happen when your dad goes to be with the Lord? Who's going to pastor the church?" My father had never designated or trained a successor. Over the years, he tried many times to get me to minister, but I didn't think that was in me. I'd never ministered or been to seminary.

When my father went to be with the Lord in 1999, in the back of my mind I thought that God would send us a senior pastor with a dynamic personality and a booming voice and several academic degrees behind his name. I was looking around, thinking, *Where is he?* The whole time, on the inside I could hear that still small voice saying, "Joel, you've spent your whole life celebrating others. Now it's time for you to be celebrated and to step up to a new level of your destiny. This is your time. This is your moment. The promise is in you." I said, "God, I don't have the booming voice. I don't have the dynamic personality. I don't have the degrees." God said, "Joel, I formed you before the foundation of the world. I put in you everything that you need. I wouldn't ask you to do it if you didn't already have what it takes."

All of a sudden I had a strong desire to step up and pastor the church. I always knew that God would take care of the church after my dad was gone, but I never dreamed it would be through me. I thought the promise would happen some other way, but I discovered the promise was in me.

God is saying the same thing to you. You've celebrated others. Now it's time to celebrate yourself. It's time for you to think better thoughts about yourself. It's time for you to shine. There is a seed on the inside just waiting to flourish. You may not feel as though you can do it, but God would not have given you the opportunity unless He had already equipped and empowered you. You have everything you need.

God will never ask you for something without first putting it in you. When God gives you a dream, when you have a desire and you know you're supposed to take a step of faith, you may feel completely unqualified. You may tell yourself that you don't have the wisdom, the know-how, or the ability to take the step. But if you'll dare to take that step, just as I did, you'll discover things in you that you never knew you had. I never knew the gift to minister was in me. I never knew that I could get up in front of people and minister to them. I wonder how many gifts are in you right now just waiting to be released.

Consider This

This is where Sarah, Abraham's wife, almost missed it. She had the promise of God, but because she thought it was impossible for her to give birth to a child, she thought it would come through somebody else. Have you responded to a promise God has put in you in a manner similar to Sarah? How did it work out?

What the Scriptures Say

For God did not give us a spirit of timidity *or* cowardice *or* fear, but [He has given us a spirit] of power and of love and of sound judgment *and* personal discipline [abilities that result in a calm, well-balanced mind and self-control].

2 TIMOTHY 1:7 AMP

I can do all things [which He has called me to do] through Him who strengthens *and* empowers me [to fulfill His purpose—I am self-sufficient in Christ's sufficiency; I am ready for anything and equal to anything through Him who infuses me with inner strength and confident peace.]

PHILIPPIANS 4:13 AMP

Thoughts for Today

If we did all the things we are capable of, we would literally astound ourselves.

THOMAS EDISON

Don't assume you have to be extraordinary to be used by God. You don't have to have exceptional gifts, talents, abilities, or connections. God specializes in using ordinary people whose limitations and weaknesses make them ideal showcases for His greatness and glory.

NANCY LEIGH DEMOSS

Courage is a door that can only be opened from the inside.

TERRY NEIL

A Prayer for Today

Father, thank You that I didn't get left out when You were handing out the gifts, the talents, or the looks. Thank You that You chose me just the way I am and put something special in me that will cause me to shine. I believe that I will give birth to the promise You placed in my heart, and that You have given me everything that I need to do it. In Jesus' Name. Amen.

TakeawayTruth

What God has placed in your heart is not going to come to pass through your neighbor, your cousin, your coworker, or your friend. God is saying, "I've anointed you. I've equipped you. I've breathed My life into you." Now quit looking for somebody else. Quit thinking that you don't have what it takes. You've been chosen by the Creator of the universe. You don't need anyone else to give birth to the promise that God put in your heart.

CHAPTER TWELVE

A Fire Shut Up in Your Bones

Key Truth

You may be at a place where you can easily be discouraged and give up on what God has placed in your heart. But the good news is that the promise God has spoken over you will not die. Deep down, you'll feel a burning, a restlessness, a fire. That's the promise God has put in you. God loves you too much to let you remain average. He's going to push you into greatness.

Caleb and Joshua were two of the twelve men whom Moses sent in to spy out the Promised Land. They came back and said, "We are well able to take the land; let us go in at once." They knew the promise was in them, but the other ten spies' negative report convinced the entire nation of Israel that they could not defeat their enemies, and they never did enter the Promised Land.

Forty years later, when Caleb was eighty-five years old, he was still fired up about not making it into the Promised Land. He knew the promise was still in him. He went back to the place he'd been forty years earlier, the place where the others would not go, and he declared, "Give me this mountain." What's interesting is that this mountain had three fierce giants living on it—the giants the other ten spies said made them feel like grasshoppers. It would have been a lot easier to ask for a mountain with less opposition, but Caleb's attitude was, *God, this is what You promised me, and I'm not going to settle for mediocrity when I know You put greatness in me. Yes, I'm older; yes, it's been a long time. I've gone through disappointments. But the promise is in me.* At eighty-five years old, he drove out the giants, took the mountain, and saw the dream come to pass.

Similarly in the Scripture, God put a promise in Jeremiah that he would be a prophet and speak to the nations. Jeremiah was young, afraid, and didn't think he could do it. People and obstacles came against him. He got so discouraged that he was about to give up. Jeremiah began to list one complaint after another: "God, these people are mocking me. When I speak, they make fun of me. I'm being ridiculed. I'm tired. I'm lonely. I'm intimidated." Jeremiah had a long list.

But just when you thought Jeremiah was going to quit, he said, "[God, Your] word is in my heart like a fire, a fire shut up in my bones" (Jer. 20:9). He was saying, "God, I don't see how it can happen. All the odds are against me. But this promise You put in me will not go away. It's like fire. It's like a burning. I can't get away from it." When Jeremiah began to think better and let the fire burn, his life passion was restored.

You may be at a place where you can easily be discouraged and give up on what God has placed in your heart. You may think it's been too long. You're too old. But the good news is, as was true for Jeremiah, there is a fire shut up in your bones. There is a promise that God has spoken over you that will not die. You can try to ignore it. Your mind or others will try to convince you it's never going to happen. But deep down, you'll feel a burning, a restlessness, a fire. That's the promise God put in you. God loves you too much to let you remain average. He's going to push you into greatness. You're going to accomplish more than you thought possible. You're going to go further than you dreamed. You're going to see the exceeding greatness of God's power. What He's spoken over your life will come to pass.

Consider This

Each of us faces times of discouragement about fulfilling what God has put in our heart. What can you draw from Caleb's declaration and Jeremiah's confession to help you accomplish more than you ever dreamed possible?

What the Scriptures Say

That is why I remind you to fan into flame the gracious
gift of God, [that inner fire—the special endowment]
which is in you through the laying on of my hands
[with those of the elders at your ordination].

2 TIMOTHY 1:6 AMP

"Fear not, for I *am* with you; be not dismayed, for I *am*
your God. I will strengthen you, yes, I will help you,
I will uphold you with My righteous right hand."

ISAIAH 41:10 NKJV

Thoughts for Today

If I had to select one quality, one personal characteristic that I regard as being most highly correlated with success, whatever the field, I would pick the trait of persistence. Determination. The will to endure to the end, to get knocked down seventy times and get up off the floor saying, "Here comes number seventy-one!"

RICHARD DEVOS

You may have had a rough start, but your story is not over. Don't allow your past, your hurt, or your tragedy to define your future. You can do it. God is on your side, and He will direct your steps throughout every part of your journey.

DODIE OSTEEN

Give me the love that leads the way, the faith that nothing can dismay, the hope no disappointments tire, the passion that will burn like fire; let me not sink to be a clod: make me Thy fuel, Flame of God.

AMY CARMICHAEL

A Prayer for Today

Father God, thank You that the promise You have spoken
over me will not die. Thank You that You love me too much
to let me remain average or to settle and that You are pushing
me into greatness. I believe that You have placed a passion
within me and that You will take me further than I
ever dreamed possible. In Jesus' Name. Amen.

TakeawayTruth

You may be facing big challenges, things are coming against you. That's a sign you're about to see a dream come to pass. Now is not the time to get discouraged. Now is the time to dig your heels in and declare, "I am in it to win it. I know the promise is in me. I'm not going to let this disappointment, this setback, or this person steal my destiny. I'm going to give birth to everything that God has placed in my heart."

RELEASE

ASK

CROWN

REMOVE

POSSIBILITIES

REPROGRAM

THINK

PROMISES

REMEMBER

SECTION VII

Ask Big

CHAPTER THIRTEEN

More Than Enough

Key Truth

When God laid out the plan for your life, He didn't just put into it what you need to get by to survive. He put more than enough in it. He's a God of abundance. We see this all throughout the Scripture. David said, "My cup overflows" (Ps. 23:5). He had an abundance, more than he needed. God wants you to have an abundance, so you can be a blessing to those around you. That's the God we serve.

2/14/19

All through the Scripture we see that our God is a God of abundance. After Jesus multiplied the little boy's lunch of five loaves of bread and two fish, thousands of people ate, and yet there were twelve basketfuls of leftovers. It is interesting that they had counted the people beforehand, so Jesus knew how many people were in the crowd that day. If He had wanted to be exact, He could have made just enough so there would be no leftovers. On purpose, He made more than enough. That's the God we serve. *2/14/19*

This is where the Israelites missed it. They had been in slavery for so many years that they became conditioned to not having enough, to barely getting by. When Pharaoh got upset with Moses, he told his foremen to have the Israelites make the same amount of bricks without the straw being provided for them. I'm sure the Israelites prayed, "God, please, help us to make our quotas and to find the supplies that we need." They prayed from a slave mentality, from a limited mind-set. Instead of asking to be freed from their oppressors, they were asking to become better slaves. Instead of praying for what God promised them, the land flowing with milk and honey, they prayed that God would help them function better in their dysfunction.

Are you asking today to become a better slave or are you asking for the abundant, overflowing, more-than-enough life that God has for you? God says you are to reign in life, that whatever you touch will prosper and succeed. Don't pray to just get by, to endure. Dare to ask big. Ask for what God has promised you. The medical report may not look good. That's okay. There's another report: "God, You said You would restore health back to me. You said the number of my days, You will fulfill." Maybe you've gone through a disappointment, a bad break. Don't pray, "God, help me to deal with this loneliness." That's a slave mentality. Turn it around with some better thoughts: "God, You said you would give me beauty for these ashes, joy for this mourning, and that You would pay me back double for this unfair situation." Or your dream may look impossible. You don't see how it can work out: "God, You said Your blessings would chase me down, that I'm surrounded by favor, that goodness and mercy are following me, and that you would give me the desires of my heart."

God can make things happen that you could never make happen. He's already placed abundance in your future. He's already lined up the right people, the breaks you need, doors to open that you could never open. My question is, "Are you asking big?" Or are you letting your circumstances—how you were raised, what somebody said—talk you out of it? If you go through life praying only "barely getting by" prayers, you'll miss the fullness of your destiny.

Take the limits off God and ask big, not from a slave mentality, not from a limited mind-set. Don't ask God to help you function better in your dysfunction. Ask God to help you think bigger and better so you can live better. Ask Him for your dreams. Ask Him for new levels. Ask Him for explosive blessings. Ask Him to propel you into your purpose.

Consider This

Matthew 20 records the story of two blind men who started shouting, "Jesus, have mercy on us!" Jesus asked them, "What do you want me to do for you?" (v. 32). If Jesus were to ask you the same thing, how would you answer? (He is asking you that, by the way, and how you answer is going to have a great impact on what God does.)

What the Scriptures Say

You do not have because you do not ask God.

JAMES 4:2

And my God will liberally supply (fill until full) your every
need according to His riches in glory in Christ Jesus.

PHILIPPIANS 4:19 AMP

Thoughts for Today

Jesus Christ opens wide the doors of the treasure house
of God's promises and bids us go in and take with
boldness the riches that are ours.

CORRIE TEN BOOM

Pray for great things, expect great things, work for
great things, but above all, pray.

R. A. TORREY

God will either give you what you ask, or something far better.

ROBERT MURRAY MCCHEYNE

A Prayer for Today

Father in heaven, thank You that You are a God of abundance
and that You have an abundant, overflowing, more-than-
enough life for me. Help me to take the limits off You and
to ask big, to ask You for my dreams and explosive blessings.
I believe that You will help me to reign in life and to
be a difference maker so I can be a blessing to those
around me. In Jesus' Name. Amen.

TakeawayTruth

God is for you. He is more powerful than
any force that's trying to stop you. When
you ask big, God calls that a healthy
prayer. He knows how to make up for
what you didn't get. Ask in spite of what
the circumstances look like or what people
are telling you. Ask to be the difference
maker. Ask to set a new standard. Take the
limits off God. Ask big. This is the year for
God to accelerate His goodness, to propel
you into your destiny.

CHAPTER FOURTEEN

Today Is Your Birthday

Key Truth

God said in Psalm 2 MSG: "You're my son, and today is your birthday. What do you want? Name it: Nations as a present? Continents as a prize?" Notice how big God thinks. We're praying for a promotion; God's talking about giving us nations. We're praying to pay our bills; God's planning on blessing us so we can pay other people's bills. We're looking at loaves and fish; God's thinking about basketfuls of leftovers.

What does that mean when God says, "Today is your birthday"? On your birthday, more than at any other time, you feel entitled to ask for something out of the ordinary. Over time, as we get older, our enthusiasm may go down a little, but think back to when you were a child. You knew that was your special day. You had the boldness to ask for what you really wanted.

God is saying, "When you pray, act as though it's your birthday. Come to Me with a boldness. Ask Me for what you really want. Don't be shy. Don't hold back. Tell Me your dreams. Tell Me what you're believing for. Ask for the secret things I placed in your heart."

Too often, instead of approaching God as though it's our birthday, believing that He'll do something special, we do just the opposite. "Joel, I can't ask for what I really want. That wouldn't be right. That would be greedy. That would be selfish."

Consider what Solomon did. In Psalm 72, he prayed what seemed to be a very self-centered prayer. He asked God to make him well-known, that his fame would spread throughout the land, that the wealth and honor of other nations would be brought to him, and that kings and queens would bow down before him. You would think God would say, "Solomon, what's wrong with you? I'm not going to make you famous. I'm not going to give you this honor, wealth, and influence. You need to learn some humility." But God didn't rebuke him. God didn't tell him he was selfish and greedy. God did exactly what he asked for. Solomon became one of the most famous people of his day. The queen of Sheba came, bowed down before him, and brought him gold and silver.

Here's the key: The reason God answered that bold prayer is because Solomon went on to pray, "God, if You'll make my name famous, if You'll give me influence and wealth, I will use it to help the widows, to take care of the orphans, to bring justice to the oppressed, to give a voice to those who don't have any voice." He asked big, not just so he would look impressive, drive the fanciest chariot, and live in the biggest palace. It was so he could lift the fallen, restore the broken, and help the hurting to advance God's kingdom. God has no problem giving you influence, honor, wealth, and even fame, as long as your dream, in some way, is connected to helping others, to making this world a better place. When your thoughts align with God's thoughts for others, He will help make your life better.

God is raising up a new generation of Solomons, people who have the boldness to say, "God, make me famous in my field. Let my gifts and talents stand out. Let my work be so excellent, so inspiring, that people all around me know who I am, not for my glory, but so I can use my influence to advance Your kingdom." Whatever field you're in—medicine, sales, construction, accounting, teaching—I dare you to pray, "God, make me famous in my field. Let me shine. Give me influence." There's no limit to what God will do for you if you'll use what He's given you to help others.

Consider This

What does "Today is your birthday" mean to you when
God says it? Do you come to Him in prayer as though it is your
birthday? What difference would it make if you approached every
new day with the belief that God has made it your birthday?

I like this today is really my actual
birthday 4/10 My children except one remembered
it only Jcerl my youngest the blessing on
and his wife & baby in Jesus name

What the Scriptures Say

Ask me, and I will make the nations your inheritance,
the ends of the earth your possession.

PSALM 2:8

I *am* the LORD your God, who brought you up out of Egypt;
open wide your mouth, and I will fill it.

PSALM 81:10 NKJV

Thoughts for Today

Prayer is not overcoming God's reluctance: it is laying
hold of His highest willingness.

RICHARD CHENEVIX TRENCH

More things are wrought by prayer than this world dreams of.

ALFRED LORD TENNYSON

Prayer moves the hand that moves the world.

JOHN A. WALLACE

A Prayer for Today

Father, thank You for the amazing promise that it is Your
good pleasure to give me the kingdom and to see me step up
to become who I was created to be. Thank You that You say
today is my birthday, and tomorrow is my birthday, and that
I can come to You with boldness. I believe that You are
going to give me influence as I use what You've given
me to help others. In Jesus' Name. Amen.

TakeawayTruth

Go to God with childlike faith as though it's your birthday, believing that He'll do something special. Ask Him for your dreams. Jesus said, "...it is your Father's good pleasure to give you the kingdom" (Luke 12:32 NKJV). Nothing makes God happier than for Him to see you step up to become who you were created to be. God is going to give you more influence, more resources, and more notoriety. You're going to accomplish your dreams and rise higher than you ever thought possible.

ASK

RELEASE

CROWN

REMOVE

POSSIBILITIES

THINK

PROMISES

REPROGRAM

REMEMBER

SECTION VIII

You Have What You Need

CHAPTER FIFTEEN

Much, Much More

Key Truth

So often we think, *If I had more money...If I had a bigger house... If I had more talent, I could be happy and do something great.* But as long as you feel as though you're lacking, you'll make excuses to be less than your best. You have to get a new perspective. God has given you exactly what you need for the season you're in. You have the talent, the friends, the connections, the resources, and the experience you need for right now.

Psalm 34:10 says, "Those who seek the LORD lack no good thing." Because your trust is in the Lord, you don't have to worry. Whatever you need, God will make sure you have it when you need it. You won't lack any good thing. This means that if you don't have it right now, don't be discouraged. You don't need it right now. Our attitude should be, *I'm equipped, empowered, and anointed for this moment. I am not lacking, shortchanged, inadequate, missing out, or less than. I have what I need for today.*

This approach is so much better than thinking, *If I just had the finances...If the loan would have gone through...If she would have been my friend...If I had a better personality...* If you needed a better personality, God would have given you a better personality. God wasn't having a bad day when He created you. If you needed more talent, God would have given you more talent. If you needed more friends, you would have more friends. Take what you have and make the most of it. It's what you need for right now.

"If I just had more money..." If you needed more money to fulfill your destiny right now and God withheld it, He wouldn't be a just God. The truth is, God has already lined up the right people, the right opportunities, the finances, the wisdom, the good breaks, and the protection you need. It's in your future. As long as you keep honoring God, He will give you what you need when you need it. That means if you don't have it right now, you don't need it right now. If you will be faithful where you are now, knowing that you have exactly what you need for the season that you're in, God will get you to where you're supposed to be.

In the book of 2 Samuel 12 is the story of how King David got off course with his life. The prophet Nathan was correcting him. In doing so, he reminded David that he had experienced God's goodness, favor, protection, provision, and healing down through the years. God made an interesting statement through Nathan: "[David,] if that had not been enough, I would have given you much, much more" (v. 8 NLT). In other words, "David, looking back over your life, if you were ever lacking, if you ever needed more wisdom, more favor, more protection, or more finance, God would have given it to you."

That tells me that what I have right now is what I need to fulfill my destiny. The moment it becomes insufficient is the moment God will give me more. The moment something starts to keep you from your destiny, the moment it begins to stop God's plan for your life, is the moment God will show up, the moment He will intervene. So if it hasn't happened yet, you haven't needed it. When you need it, it won't be one second late. The moment you need a new friend, a good break, or an idea, it will show up. God is closely watching your life. You are His most prized possession. He is saying to you what He said to David: "If it's ever not enough, you can count on Me. I will always be there to give you more."

Consider This

Do you believe that for the season of life you are now in that you have exactly what you need? What changes can you make in what you tell yourself that will empower you to live not feeling you are lacking or shortchanged?

What the Scriptures Say

I have learned in whatever state I am, to be content: I know how to be abased, and I know how to abound. Everywhere and in all things I have learned both to be full and to be hungry, both to abound and to suffer need. I can do all things through Christ who strengthens me.

PHILIPPIANS 4:11–13 NKJV

"I will give you hidden treasures, riches stored in secret places, so that you may know that I am the LORD, the God of Israel, who summons you by name."

ISAIAH 45:3

Thoughts for Today

Do not spoil what you have by desiring what you have not;
remember that what you now have was once among
the things you only hoped for.

EPICURUS

So [God] supplies perfectly measured grace to meet the needs
of the godly. For daily needs there is daily grace; for sudden
needs, sudden grace; for overwhelming need, overwhelming
grace. God's grace is given wonderfully, but not wastefully;
freely but not foolishly; bountifully but not blindly.

JOHN BLANCHARD

God has great things in store for His people;
they ought to have large expectations.

C. H. SPURGEON

A Prayer for Today

Father God, thank You that You have given me exactly
what I need for the season I am in. Thank You that I have
the talent, the friends, the connections, the resources, and the
experience I need for right now. I believe that You know what
I need and when I need it, and You know how to get it to me.
As long as I am honoring You, whatever I need will find me,
and it won't be a second late. In Jesus' Name. Amen.

TakeawayTruth

God has you in the palm of His hands.
He knows what you need and when you
need it, and He knows how to get it to
you. If you don't have something right
now, God didn't forget about you. As long
as you're honoring Him, at the right time,
when you need them, the right people
will show up. When you need it, the
finances will come. When you need it,
the healing, the restoration, and the
vindication will find you.

CHAPTER SIXTEEN

Do Not Despise Small Beginnings

Key Truth

Do not underestimate what you have. It may look small and insignificant. Compared to what you're facing, perhaps it seems utterly useless. But when God breathes on your life, the odds dramatically change. You and God are a majority. God can take you beyond where your talent and your education say you should be. If you will be confident in what God has given you, He can take what looks like little and turn it into much.

echariah 4:10 says that we should not "despise the day of small things." In other words, don't look at what you have and say, "I can't do anything great. I don't have a lot of talent." What God has given you right now may seem small, but don't let that fool you. When you use what you have, God will multiply it. You will see an explosion of His goodness.

Samson was surrounded by a huge army. Everywhere he looked there were horses, chariots, and weapons. All he had was the jawbone of a donkey. No weapon. No armor. Nobody was backing him up. But he picked up that jawbone, God breathed on him, and he defeated an army of a thousand men. All Moses had was an ordinary stick, something he found on the ground, yet when he picked up that rod and held it in the air, the Red Sea supernaturally parted. All my father had when he started Lakewood was ninety people and an abandoned, run-down feed store, yet God breathed on them and did something extraordinary.

When David went out to face Goliath, King Saul tried to get David to wear his armor. David didn't have any protection, and his only weapon was his slingshot. Saul had good intentions. He said, "David, at least wear my armor. You're going to go out there and get killed." However, David was much smaller than King Saul, and when he put that armor on, it swallowed him. It didn't help him. It weighed him down. That's because what God has given other people is not going to work for you. Don't try to be like somebody else. "I wish I had their talent, their looks, their personality." If you put that armor on, you would be uncomfortable, just as David was. It would slow you down. Why? It wasn't designed for you. You are one of a kind. God has custom-made your armor. Nobody has what you have. When you go out today, you need to walk with some swag!

David took that armor off and said, "No, thanks. This is not for me. I can't be who God created me to be by wearing somebody else's armor. I have what I need." It may not be as much as somebody else has—you may have less talent, less resources, and fewer friends—but if you'll walk in your own anointing, if you'll use what God has given you, you will go further than people who have more talent and more resources, because God is breathing on your life. That's what happened with David. He defeated Goliath with less equipment. Goliath was wearing a full set of armor and had a huge spear. All David had was the slingshot. The difference was that the slingshot was a part of David's divine destiny. If he had looked at it and thought, *It's nothing. It's small. It's insignificant. I can't do this,* he would have missed his destiny.

Get up every morning and remind yourself, "I have the strength, the talent, the friends, the resources, and the qualifications I need for today." If you'll do that, because your trust is in the Lord, God is going to take the small and turn it into much. He is going to multiply what you have and take you places you've never dreamed possible.

Consider This

The Scripture tells of four starving lepers who were marching toward an enemy's camp. God multiplied the sound of their footsteps to sound like a huge army was attacking. The lepers had nothing but their footsteps. What do you have? How does what they had compare to what you have as regards the fulfilling of your dream?

....

....

....

....

....

....

....

....

....

....

....

....

....

....

....

....

....

What the Scriptures Say

"He who is faithful in a very little thing is also faithful
in much; and he who is dishonest in a very little
thing is also dishonest in much."

LUKE 16:10 AMP

"Your servant has nothing there at all," she said, "except a
small jar of olive oil." Elisha said, "Go around and ask all your
neighbors for empty jars. Don't ask for just a few. Then go
inside and shut the door behind you and your sons. Pour oil
into all the jars, and as each is filled, put it to one side." They
brought the jars to her and she kept pouring. When all the
jars were full…the oil stopped flowing.

2 KINGS 4:2–6

Thoughts for Today

There is nothing small if God is in it.

DWIGHT L. MOODY

So never lose an opportunity of urging a practical beginning, however small, for it is wonderful how often in such matters the mustard seed germinates and roots itself.

FLORENCE NIGHTINGALE

One on God's side is a majority.

WENDELL PHILLIPS

A Prayer for Today

Father in heaven, thank You that the gifts, the talents, the looks, and the personality You have given me were custom-made for me alone. Thank You that You put in me exactly what I need to fulfill Your plan for my life. I believe that as I use what I have, even what seems small and insignificant, You are going to take it and multiply it into something extraordinary. In Jesus' Name. Amen.

TakeawayTruth

You may not have the talent, the looks, the personality, the income, or the influence that somebody else has. But what God has given you was custom-made for you alone. He specifically gave you your gifts, your talents, your looks, and your personality. God didn't close His eyes and say, "Here, just take this. It will do." No, God matched you for your world. He put in you exactly what you need to fulfill His plan for your life.

Keep Your Crown

CHAPTER SEVENTEEN

The Crown of Honor Is Yours

Key Truth

When God breathed His life into you, He put "a crown of glory and honor" on your head (Ps. 8:5). This crown represents your authority. It's a reminder that you are royalty. When you're wearing your crown, you'll have a sense of entitlement, thinking, *I have a right to be blessed and to overcome these challenges—not because I'm so great or so talented, but because I'm wearing a crown of honor put there by my Creator.*

our perception of yourself will determine what kind of life you live. If you think of yourself as being average, if you feel less-than because of what somebody said about you, if you live with guilt and condemnation because of past mistakes, that's going to limit your potential. What's happening? You're not wearing your crown of honor and glory.

Jesus said, "Hold on to what you have, so that no one will take your crown" (Rev. 3:11). Throughout life, there will always be someone or something trying to take your crown. People will talk about you, trying to make you look bad, to push you down. What they're really doing is trying to get your crown. Don't let them have it. Nobody can take your crown. You have to let go of what was said or done to you rather than let go of your crown.

When somebody tries to make you feel small, they make derogatory statements. Instead of being upset and believing what they say, just reach up and straighten your crown. They can't change who you are unless you allow them to. They don't control your destiny. They don't determine your value. They didn't breathe life into you; God did. He calls you a masterpiece. He says you're a king, a queen. You're supposed to reign in life. That's why He put the crown of honor on your head. It's to remind you of who you are.

The mistake we make too often is to believe the lies. Somebody says, "You're not that talented." Instead of saying, "No, thanks," we say, "Oh, you're right. Let me take off my crown. I thought I was talented." The message comes to us: "You're not royalty. You come from the wrong family. You'll never do anything great." Instead of ignoring it, not giving it the time of day, we think, *What was I thinking? Let me take off my crown.*

The enemy's main tool is deception. There's nothing he would love more than for you to go through life not wearing your crown, letting people and circumstances convince you that "You don't deserve to be blessed. You don't have what it takes. You've been through too much. You can't feel good about yourself."

Jesus said to His critics, "Your approval means nothing to Me" (John 5:41 NLT). That's a powerful way to live. He was saying, "I know who I am, and nothing you do or don't do is going to change Me. You can celebrate Me or you can crucify Me, but I'm keeping My crown." People are impulsive. One moment they can be cheering for you, as they did with Jesus, and another moment they can be putting you down, trying to make you look bad.

If wearing your crown is based on whether or not people like you, whether or not they believe in you, you're going to be taking your crown off and then putting it back on throughout your whole life. You don't need other people's approval; you have Almighty God's approval. Our attitude should be, *You can be for me or against me, you can celebrate me or criticize me, but one thing is for certain: I'm not giving you my crown. I know who I am. I am royalty. I am accepted. I am approved. I am valuable.*

Consider This

What have people said or what thoughts do you have that try to take away your crown? What better thoughts will counter those negative words or thoughts and keep you free from others carrying away your blessing?

What the Scriptures Say

For if, by the trespass of the one man, death reigned through
that one man, how much more will those who receive God's
abundant provision of grace and of the gift of righteousness
reign in life through the one man, Jesus Christ!

ROMANS 5:17

Praise the LORD, my soul, and forget not all his benefits—
who forgives all your sins and heals all your diseases,
who redeems your life from the pit and crowns you
with love and compassion…

PSALM 103:2–4

Thoughts for Today

No one can make you feel inferior without your permission.

ELEANOR ROOSEVELT

Don't seek to be a people pleaser…don't compromise
what you know is right in your heart to gain the approval
of others. The only approval you need is God's,
and you already have that.

JOYCE MEYER

Satan's purpose is to take from you what God has given to you.

JOHN OSTEEN

A Prayer for Today

Father, thank You that when You breathed Your life into me,
You put a crown of glory and honor on my head. Thank You
that You have crowned me as royalty and that I don't need
other people to approve of me. I believe that I have a right
to be blessed and to overcome challenges for the simple
reason that I am Your child and no one can take my
crown from me. In Jesus' Name. Amen.

TakeawayTruth

Don't you dare give away your crown! It belongs to you. It was put there by your Creator. It has nothing to do with how you feel, how you look, or what other people say. It's based solely on the fact that you are a child of the Almighty God. He has crowned you with glory and honor. Keep believing. Keep hoping. Keep pursuing. You don't need everyone to be for you. You and God are a majority.

CHAPTER EIGHTEEN

The Crown Gives You Favor

Key Truth

The enemy has been trying to get our crown from the beginning of time. In the Garden of Eden, Adam and Eve were living confident and secure, at peace with God, at peace with themselves. They were wearing their crowns of God's favor. But one day the enemy deceived them into eating the forbidden fruit. When they did, immediately they were afraid and ashamed. In effect, they gave the enemy their crowns.

When you're wearing your crown of God's favor, you are confident and secure. You know you're a masterpiece, one of a kind, a prized possession. You're not dwelling on all the negative chatter—what you're not, what you don't have, or what other people are saying. You go through the day with a smile on your face and a spring in your step. You know you're royalty, that you've been crowned with glory and honor. When you think this way, you will live this way, and you're going to come into divine connections.

When we surrender our crown of honor and favor, as Adam and Eve did, it opens the door to fear, insecurity, and shame. We focus on what we're not, on the mistakes we've made, on what other people have said about us. Where there's no crown, there's no covering. There's no reminder of who we are. We believe those lies that can push us down.

When God came looking for Adam and Eve, He asked, "Who told you that you were naked?" God is asking us today, "Who told you there's something wrong with you? Who told you you're just average? That you can't accomplish your dreams? That you're not good enough?" I can assure you those negative thoughts didn't come from our God. You need to put your crown back on. You may have let some person or some event take it. The good news is that you can get it back. It's not too late; you have control over your crown.

In the Scripture, a woman named Naomi first lost her husband in death, then both her married sons died as well. She was so discouraged that she thought, *I'm done. I'll never be happy again.* She took off her crown. She had been a happy woman, but now she was bitter. She even changed her name from Naomi, which means "my joy," to Mara, which means "bitter." She was saying, "Call me bitter." The problem is that when you take off your crown, you take off the favor, the honor, and the glory. In tough times like hers, more than ever, you need to keep reminding yourself, "I am a child of the Most High God. I am extremely valuable. God has beauty for these ashes; double is coming my way."

Naomi's widowed daughter-in-law Ruth met a man named Boaz, and they married. One day they had a little baby boy. Naomi had thought her life was finished, but when she saw that little baby, something came alive on the inside. The Scripture says, "The women in the town rejoiced, saying, 'Naomi, God has given you a son. This baby will restore your youth.'" She felt a new sense of purpose. She took care of that little baby as though he were her own. Naomi thought she'd never be happy again, but now she was more fulfilled than ever. That was God paying her back for the unfair things that had happened—she had her crown back on.

Nothing that's happened to you has stopped God's plan. He knows how to give beauty for ashes, how to turn mourning into dancing. As Naomi did, you may have taken your crown off, thinking that you've seen your best days, but you need to get ready. God still has a purpose for you to fulfill. He still has something amazing in your future. Put your crown back on.

Consider This

You a child of the Most High God, crowned with honor and glory. Do you struggle with forgetting who you are, or do you feel the pressure to reprogram your thinking to be less than a king or queen? Write out power thoughts for how you will keep your crown on, no matter what life brings.

What the Scriptures Say

But I am afraid that just as Eve was deceived by the serpent's
cunning, your minds may somehow be led astray from
your sincere and pure devotion to Christ.

2 CORINTHIANS 11:3

...to bestow on them a crown of beauty instead of ashes, the
oil of joy instead of mourning, and a garment of praise instead
of a spirit of despair. They will be called oaks of righteousness,
a planting of the LORD for the display of his splendor.

ISAIAH 61:3

Thoughts for Today

Despondency does not become a prince, much less a Christian. Our God is "the God of hope," and we should hope in Him. We should hope in His mercy, in His patience, in His provision, in His plenteous redemption. We should hope for light in darkness; for strength in weakness; for direction in perplexity; for deliverance in danger; for victory in conflict, and for triumph in death.

JAMES SMITH

Why believe the devil instead of believing God? Rise up and realize the truth about yourself—that all the past has gone, and you are one with Christ, and all your sins have been blotted out once and forever. O let us remember that it is sin to doubt God's Word. It is sin to allow the past, which God has dealt with, to rob us of our joy and our usefulness in the present and in the future.

MARTYN LLOYD-JONES

The God who made us also can remake us.

WOODROW KROLL

....

....

....

....

....

....

....

A Prayer for Today

Father God, thank You that because You have crowned me with Your favor, I can be confident and secure, knowing that I am Your prized possession. Thank You that I can put aside the negative chatter about what I am not, what I don't have, and what other people are saying about me. I believe that nothing that's happened in the past or anything that happens in the future can take my crown away or stop Your plan from being fulfilled in my life. In Jesus' Name. Amen.

TakeawayTruth

Maybe you've been through a disappointment, a loss, something didn't work
out. It would be easy for you to feel not
valuable, not excited about life. Put your
crown back on. That crown is what gives
you the favor. The crown is what causes
you to stand out. Nothing that's happened
has lessened your value. You are still the
prized possession, the apple of God's eye.
Don't let a disappointment or a loss carry
away your blessing. It's not the end. It's a
new beginning.

RELEASE
CROWN
REMOVE
ASK
POSSIBILITIES
REPROGRAM
REMEMBER
THINK
PROMISES

SECTION X

Just Remember

CHAPTER NINETEEN

Develop the Habit of Remembering

Key Truth

When you look back over your life, consider some of the things you've faced that at the time you didn't think you could make it through. The obstacle was so large, the breakup hurt you so badly, the medical report was so negative. You didn't see a way, but God turned it around. He gave you strength when you didn't think you could go on. That wasn't a lucky break. It was the hand of God.

When the Israelites came out of slavery in Egypt untrained for battle and with no military training or weapons, God said to them in Deuteronomy 7, "You may think, 'How can we conquer these nations that are much stronger than us?' But don't be afraid. Just remember what I did to Pharaoh. You saw the miraculous signs and power I used to bring you out." God was saying, "When it looks impossible, the way to stay encouraged and keep your hopes up is to remember what God has done."

As was true for the Israelites, we have seen with our own eyes those times when God made a way. When you face tough times and your dream looks impossible, just remember. Go back and replay your victories. You thought you were stuck, but God opened a door. You faced the loss of a loved one, and you thought you would never be happy again, but God turned your mourning into dancing. Remember how He put you at the right place at the right time. Remember how He spared your life from that accident.

If you're going to overcome obstacles, if you're going to reach your highest potential, you have to learn to remember. When you're constantly thinking about God's goodness, how He's protected you, vindicated you, and promoted you, not only will faith rise in your heart, but it's that attitude of expectancy that allows God to do great things.

When the apostle Paul talks about "the mercies of God" in Romans 12:1, he doesn't use the singular but the plural. Every one of us has experienced some of these mercies. Perhaps you can join me in saying that you wouldn't be alive if it wasn't for God's mercies. Some of the things you've done—the crowds you used to run with, the drugs, the alcohol, the reckless driving, the freak accidents—should have taken you out. But God showed you some of His mercies—not once, but again and again.

Maybe you shouldn't have the position you're in at your workplace. You weren't the most qualified, but the mercies of God gave it to you. Or perhaps that sickness said it was going to be the end, but the mercies of God said, "This is not your time." When you recognize what God has done, that all through your life it's been His hand getting you to where you are, then it's easy to honor God; it's easy to be grateful. It's easy to serve, to give, and to help others. You realize that where you are in life is because of the mercies of God.

Don't take God's mercies for granted. Keep them in the forefront of your mind. God has a destiny for you to fulfill. He has an assignment for you to accomplish. His mercies are never going to give up on you. His calling is irrevocable. He chose you before you could choose Him. You might as well recognize you're a marked man, a marked woman. The Creator of the universe has His hand on your life. The sooner you surrender your will to His, the better off you're going to be. You're not giving up anything. You're gaining purpose, your destiny, a life that He's designed, a life more rewarding than you ever imagined. You love Him because He first loved you.

Consider This

Describe a time or incident in your life when you experienced the mercies of God. Based upon the mercies of God, Paul adds in Romans 12:1 that we should dedicate all of ourselves to Him as "a living sacrifice." What does that mean to you?

What the Scriptures Say

And I thank Christ Jesus our Lord who has enabled me,
because He counted me faithful, putting *me* into the ministry,
although I was formerly a blasphemer, a persecutor, and an
insolent man; but I obtained mercy because I did *it* ignorantly
in unbelief. And the grace of our Lord was exceedingly
abundant, with faith and love which are in Christ Jesus.

1 TIMOTHY 1:12–14 NKJV

Look to the LORD and his strength; seek his face always.
Remember the wonders he has done, his miracles,
and the judgments he pronounced.

PSALM 105:4–5

Thoughts for Today

God's mercy is so great that you may sooner drain the sea of its water, or deprive the sun of its light, or make space too narrow, than diminish the great mercy of God.

C. H. Spurgeon

Every time you draw your breath, you suck in mercy.

Thomas Watson

God's providential hand encompasses the whole of our lives, not just the good days but the "bad" days too. We have the word *accident* in our vocabulary; He does not.

Erwin Lutzer

A Prayer for Today

Father in heaven, thank You that I can remember those times when I didn't think I could make it through situations, but You made a way when there was no way. Thank You for when You turned the impossible around and gave me the strength I needed to go on. Help me to keep Your mercies in the forefront of my mind. I surrender my will to You, and I believe that You are leading me into the life that You designed for me. In Jesus' Name. Amen.

TakeawayTruth

When you remember how God has protected you, promoted you, and restored you, faith will rise in your heart. Instead of thinking, *I'll never get out of this problem*, you'll say with confidence, "God made a way in the past; He's going to make a way in the future." Don't complain about the problem. When you come through this challenge, that victory will be the fuel you use that gets you to the next level of glory.

CHAPTER TWENTY

Remember the Right Things

Key Truth

You have a history with God. You've seen His mercies—not once, but again and again—showing out in your life. Start remembering your victories, the times God healed you, the times He promoted you, the times He stopped the accidents, the times He turned the problems around. When you're remembering the right things, you're going to move forward in faith. You'll see more of God's favor.

David said in Psalm 34, "Let all who are discouraged take heart." He goes on to tell us how to do it. "Come, let's talk about God's goodness. I prayed and the Lord answered my prayer." He was saying, "When you're discouraged, when you don't see a way out, come and let's talk about God's greatness. Let's talk about your answered prayers."

What you're saying in your tough times will make or break you. If you go around saying, "I'll never get out of this problem. It's just too big," you'll get stuck. Turn it around and say, "God, I want to thank You for Your greatness in my life. Thank You for giving me this job. Lord, thank You for freeing me from this addiction." When you're always talking about God's goodness, you won't be down and discouraged. You'll have a spring in your step, a smile on your face. You'll know that God has done it for you in the past, and He'll do it for you again in the future.

Everywhere you go, talk about God's goodness—not bragging about yourself, but bragging about what God has done. I must have heard my father tell the story a thousand times of how he gave his life to Christ. It happened when he was seventeen, but at seventy-five years old he was still telling it as though it happened just yesterday. He never lost the amazement. When you constantly think about what God has done, when you relive your miracles, when you're always in awe of His goodness, you are putting yourself in position for God to do something even more amazing.

On one occasion, the disciples were in a boat (see Mark 6). Just a few hours before, they had seen Jesus take five loaves of bread and two fish, pray over them, and feed some fifteen thousand people. At the end of that day, He told the disciples to get in the boat and cross to the other side of the lake. Now it was the middle of the night. Strong winds suddenly swept down on the lake, and the waves were very high. The disciples were concerned for their safety, when they saw Jesus walking on the water. At first, in the pitch black of night, they thought He was a ghost. They finally recognized Him and invited Him into their boat. When He got into the boat, the winds and waves calmed down immediately. They were relieved they were okay.

The Scripture tells us they were so worried because "they still didn't understand the significance of the miracle of the loaves" (v. 52 NLT). They were so stressed out by the nighttime storm and high waves, they forgot how earlier that day they had seen with their own eyes one of the greatest miracles ever recorded. If they had just remembered what God had done, if they had just remembered the miracle, they would have stayed in faith. They would have been calm, knowing that everything would be okay despite the waves.

If you are doing what they did, letting a negative circumstance cause you to live worried and stressed out, consider your miracles. Look back over your life. Remember the time God showed up and suddenly turned it around, and He'll do it for you again in the future.

Consider This

Start remembering your victories, the times God healed you, promoted you, turned the problems around. Write down three specific victories that God has worked in your life and what you want people to know about how God did them.

....
....
....
....
....
....
....
....
....
....
....
....
....
....
....
....
....
....
....

What the Scriptures Say

Surely your goodness and love will follow me all the days of my life, and I will dwell in the house of the LORD forever.

PSALM 23:6

"Yours, LORD, is the greatness and the power and the glory and the majesty and the splendor, for everything in heaven and earth is yours. Yours, LORD, is the kingdom; you are exalted as head over all."

1 CHRONICLES 29:11

Thoughts for Today

Let your fears go, lest they make you fainthearted. Stop inspiring fear in those around you and now take your stand in faith. God has been good and He will continue to manifest His goodness. Let us approach these days expecting to see the goodness of the Lord manifest. Let us be strong and of good courage, for the Lord will fight for us if we stand in faith.

Francis Frangipane

Many Christians estimate difficulties in the light of their own resources, and thus attempt little and often fail in the little they attempt. All God's giants have been weak men who did great things for God because they reckoned on His power and presence with them.

Hudson Taylor

There are no measures which can set forth the immeasurable greatness of Jehovah, who is goodness itself. If we cannot measure, we can marvel; and though we may not calculate with accuracy, we can adore with fervency.

C. H. Spurgeon

A Prayer for Today

Father, thank You for the history that I have with You and for the mercies that You have shown out in my life, not once, but again and again. Thank You that every victory You've given me wasn't just for that moment, but it was so I could remember it and use it as fuel to build my faith. I believe that as I talk about Your goodness and greatness in my life, I am putting myself in position for You to do something even more amazing. In Jesus' Name. Amen.

TakeawayTruth

How are you going to defeat the Pharaohs in your life? Just remember the right things. You have a history with God. Every victory He's given you wasn't just for that time; it was so you could go back and use that as fuel to build your faith. If you are low on faith, you need to go back and get some fuel. It's in your past victories. Don't talk about your problems; talk about the greatness of God.

STAY**CONNECTED,**
BE**BLESSED.**

From thoughtful articles to powerful blogs, podcasts and more, JoelOsteen.com is full of inspirations that will give you encouragement and confidence in your daily life.

AVAILABLE ON JOELOSTEEN.COM

 today's**W RD**

This daily devotional from Joel and Victoria will help you grow in your relationship with the Lord and equip you to be everything God intends you to be.

 **Joel Osteen STREAMING**

Miss a broadcast? Watch Joel Osteen on demand, and see Joel LIVE on Sundays.

 **Joel Osteen PODCAST**

The podcast is a great way to listen to Joel where you want, when you want.

CONNECT WITH US

Join our community of believers on your favorite social network.

TAKE HOPE WITH YOU

Get the inspiration and encouragement of Joel Osteen on your iPhone, iPad or Android device! Our app puts Joel's messages, devotions and more at your fingertips.

Thanks for helping us make a difference in the lives of millions around the world.